Turn Your Dog into a Therapy Dog

Tips from a Therapy Dog Evaluator

By:

Sally Grottini

Dedication

This book is dedicated to my Newfoundland, Second Chance at Life for taking me to interesting places that I might not ordinarily have gone and for introducing me to so many wonderful people and organizations that I may not otherwise have met. Mention must also go to my dearly departed friend Dixon Cuff. He took Chance and I under his wing and lead us both through the path of dedicating ourselves to Therapy Dog work as well as showing me what it means to be a good Therapy Dog Evaluator.

Table of Contents

Table of Contents continued

Chance and Steeler on a Billboard

~1~

Abby, February 3, 2003

Earlier on this February day it was fairly chilly, but now the sun had gone down and the evening winds had picked up slapping you in the face as you entered its path. The night's weather had proved to be too much for even a Newfoundland dog to withstand for very long.

Abby, my two year old Newfoundland, began to pace back and forth in the living room and then started to seek out every corner of the house.

"Oh no!" I said to Abby. "Not now! I am alone!"

But Abby continued to pace near the back door and became insistent that she wanted to go outside.

"Okay Abby, I said, wait just a second."

I dare not just let her out the back door alone as it could be dangerous. I grabbed a leash and attached her to the other end. She pulled and wandered aimlessly then led me into her hundred foot pen straight to the dog house where a thick bed of straw lay. She has never used a dog house, it was there only to be used if I could not get home and the weather turned bad. Even then she would go into the shed with the mattress pad that lied under the straw. She squeezed her big body into the house and turned round and round, acting uncomfortable and uncertain.

"No, Abby!" my voice raised above the wind. "Come on girl, let's go in the house."

Back inside the warm house Abby jumped up onto my son's bed. We had just redone this room for family members who would come to spend the holidays with us. Abby twirled round and round pulling at the bedspread with her teeth.

"Oh no!" I cried. "Here, right here?"

This action of Abby's sent me scrambling to the basement to gather up every old plastic tablecloth and comforter I could find. Dashing back upstairs with my arms full I saw that Abby was still twirling and pulling.

"Off Abby." I said.

Abby jumped off the bed and paced the bedroom watching me intently as I hurried to take off the new bedspread and replace it with the plastic table cloths and old bedspreads I had gathered.

"Abby, Okay!" I said once the job was done. Okay is Abby's release command, and she quickly jumped back up onto the bed and started to twirl. During her twirling I ran to the phone to call my son for help.

"Jason, can you come over?" I asked. "I think it's time!"

"I'll be right over." Jason replied, and I was thankful he lived around the corner.

~2~

The Fight for Life

Abby continued to twirl as Jason came through the back door. Just then something fell from her bottom onto the bed. It looked like a big black bubble!

"Oh, my God! Oh, my God!" I exclaimed. "That's it! That's it! That's a puppy!"

Within two more hours a second and third puppy popped out and Abby did her job very well as a new mother.

I looked at Jason. "Piece of cake!" I said. "One pup an hour gives me time to take coffee breaks!"

"Yeah, Jason replied, the dog tends to do all the work!"

By the fourth hour Abby had tired and a pup had been born but she never paid attention to it. So for at least twenty minutes that I was aware of, this pup was under Abby's big fluffy black tail unattended!

"Oh my god!" I shouted to Jason. "There's a pup and it's still in the sac not moving! Call the emergency vet, the number is on the fridge."

I quickly broke open the sac and rubbed the pup while Jason called the ER Vet, then handed me the phone.

"Hello!" I cried. "My dog has given birth to three pups that are doing well but there is a fourth pup which had been in the sac for some time and is not moving."

"Is this the dog's first litter?" the lady on the other end of the phone asked.

"Yes!" I pleaded. I felt like my heart was going to jump out of my throat.

"Okay." She replied. "You'll have to break the sac open and rub the puppy vigorously."

"I did that! I shouted. "But the pup is still not moving!"   Urgency filled my voice and tears filled my eyes as I clutched this pup wrapped in a towel to my chest.

"You'll have to try nose to mouth then." the lady said. "Have you ever done that before?"

"No!" I answered. "I've not done it, but I did read how to do it."

"Well hang up and try that with the pup, the lady advised, if nothing happens after ten minutes consider the pup gone and put it aside to tend to the other puppies. Call us back and let us know how you are doing."

I hung up the phone and gently lay my mouth over the pup's nose and mouth, breathing a few puffs very softly. Then I stopped, rubbed the pup vigorously, and repeated the procedure again.

"Oh God, I prayed, please don't let this puppy die!" I whispered between breaths. "Please help me to do this right and I swear I will keep it and it will not be just another family dog. I will do good things with this pup. Please, please, just help me!"

Four minutes passed and nothing. Five minutes, nothing. I held the pup up for another breath. Six minutes, I rubbed vigorously… nothing. Again I prayed and pleaded with God as I had done throughout this ordeal.

Seven minutes passed and another few breaths and vigorous rubbing. I cleared the pup's mouth once again with the children's aspirator in case I had missed something the first time but it felt hopeless.

"Please, please, please!" I cried.

Finally there was a very loud ewww and movement! "Oh God! Yes baby, yes baby, come on, cry, cry!" I shouted.

"Come on little pup, come on, you can do it!" Jason uttered.

And thus, Second Chance at Life was born. I marked him in red for the sign of the Red Cross and put him with his mother and siblings. Abby went on to have a total of seven pups that night when all was said and done, six boys and one girl, and that was the beginning of my date with destiny.

~3~

A Date with Second Chance

As we walked down the long dimly lit hallway the people standing in the middle making small talk began to part the way leaving me a very wide opening and I heard mutterings of, *Oh my God, he's beautiful! Look at the size of him! His long hair looks so soft and silky. Jeeze, look at the size of his feet! Look how well behaved he is!"*

"You can pet him." I said to the crowd as I moved closer to them.

Finally one brave person stepped forward to ask the questions I heard each time we greet someone new. What kind is he? A Great Dane, no a Pyrenees right? Where did you get him? How much does he weigh? What does he eat? Why is he here?"

My dog Chance, weighing one hundred and seventy five pounds, stopped directly in front of the people talking about him. He remembered his manners and the job he is here to do. He did not move, but surely if a human hand does not reach out to pet him soon he will plop down on the cool tile floor and relax.

"He is a Newfoundland, I replied. "He weighs 175 lbs and he eats anything he wants too! He is a pup from my litter of which there are four more at home, and he is a trained and certified Therapy Dog."

A gray haired man standing in the background chimed in. "You mean you have more like this at your home? This size, in the house? You must have a big house!"

"Yes, I do." I replied in a matter of fact kind of way as if everyone has such a household brood.

"What's his name?" asked a nurse who had now joined the circle surrounding Chance.

"Second Chance or just Chance for short." I replied.

"Do you call him that because he was a rescue?" the nurse asked.

"No, I said, I call him that because he died at birth and I had to give him mouth to nose to bring him back."

That one sentence usually generates a lot of oohs, ahs, and gasps out of all who meet Chance.

Within a few minutes of standing there conversing with the crowd, a mutt, about the size of Chance's paw entered through the front door and headed down the hallway. The dog is part Chihuahua and what else I am not exactly sure.

Chance began to amber forward to greet this little girl and the crowd around us watched intently.

"He'll eat that dog for a snack!" The gentleman in the crowd cried out.

"That's not enough to feed that big dog!" exclaimed the nurse.

Chance stopped dead in his tracks and put his head low to the floor as the little dog got closer to him: The crowd hushed to a whisper wondering what would happen when the two dogs met.

"Hi!" I said to the women. "And how is Bella doing today?"

"Oh, she's a pip today!" the lady replied. "Couldn't wait to get out the door!"

Bella moved quickly toward Chance and their tails wagged as they greeted each other.

Bella and Chance, although they are two very different looking dogs, have much in common: they are wearing the same red bandanna which has on it the emblem of a Therapy Dog.

What many people fail to realize is that they have the perfect Therapy Dog sitting right there in their living room! If you and your dog have an outgoing personality, enjoy being around people, and you have the time to train your dog in basic obedience and get them acclimated to objects such as canes, crutches, and wheelchairs, you are already half way there! The amount of time you choose to volunteer in Therapy Dog work is totally up to you. Who knows, one day people will be saying those very kind words as they greet you and your dog down that dimly lit hallway!

~4~

Differences between Therapy Dogs

& Assistance Dogs

As a therapy dog handler you may be asked to visit many places, but you must not abuse that privilege and pass your dog off as a needed guide dog or assistance dog, especially in places where dogs are not normally allowed. A guide or assistance dog by law is allowed anywhere if the owner needs the dog by their side to aide them in any way. Such dogs are owned by one person for the specific intent of aiding that person in their everyday life.

A Therapy Dog usually is the family dog and is trained to assist in the mental and emotional stimulation of residents in an establishment such as, but not limited to, hospitals, schools, and nursing homes. Therapy dogs are invited into establishments by a second or third party. Most recently Therapy Dogs have been brought to private homes by hospice and are being brought into disaster situations for the mental well being of people in those particular situations. The physical and mental benefits both during and after a visit from a Therapy Dog have been well documented over the years. Just the act of petting and talking to a Therapy Dog can cause a person's heart rate and blood pressure to decrease.

As well, mental and physical stimulation are increased, mood levels and vocalizations are increased, loneliness is decreased, and self esteem can be increased, especially the self esteem in young children.

With each new type of activity a Therapy Dog is invited too, new studies continue to show the positive affects they have on the people visited. For instance, in the Read to Dogs program where children gather together in groups and read a book to a dog, their reading and comprehensive skills over the year improved.

A person who might not use an arm to reach may unexpectedly use that arm to touch a therapy dog and personally I have witnessed a child who did not speak for months suddenly and within days of a visit ask this question of me. *Where's your big black dog?*

So you see, the possibilities are endless in what can be accomplished, but you must always adhere to the rules of the facility.

Today there is a vast arena of places that Therapy Dogs are used, so you don't have to limit yourself to hospitals and nursing homes and don't go into a facility that you are not totally comfortable in.

~5~

Get Started
What is needed to be a volunteer?

Getting started as a Therapy Dog volunteer basically requires time, training in obedience, and an outgoing personality by both you and your dog. A shy or aggressive dog obviously will not make a good Therapy Dog; the same would go for a human with that type of personality. A happy dog brings with it excitement to meet new people but the dog must still be under control at all times. The owner must bring with them a caring and compassionate attitude.

It is imperative that a therapy dog is acclimated to wheelchairs, crutches, canes, walkers and other medical equipment. During testing when a dog is approached by an evaluator who is using crutches the dog may be perfectly fine. When that same dog is approached with a cane the dog may go into attack mode or shy away which would result in test failure. As a trainer what I surmise is happening is that the dog is possibly recalling a bad experience with a long stick or even a cane. Since a dog from any background can be tested to become a therapy dog it's possible that if you have an adopted dog you don't know its whole history, so knowing the dog's reaction to such equipment will help you in the long run. No sense working hard in obedience and then fail the test because the dog shied away from a cane! From viewing your dog's reaction to all equipment you will gain knowledge of what further training may be needed and if you need to enlist the help of a trainer. It may also be helpful to enlist the aid of a friend to work the equipment while you work the dog. There are very few trainers per say that train specifically for Therapy Dog work like there are for guide dogs or assistance dogs, but all trainers do train basic obedience, so finding medical equipment to train your dog with will more than likely be up to you. An evaluator and trainer such as myself might have the equipment you need so there is no harm in asking about it if you enlist the help of a professional trainer. However, keep in mind you still need to do the hands on training with the dog, a trainer is only going to guide you on what to do. Why? Because if a trainer does all the work and trains the dog then the dog may only listen to commands given by that trainer, but it is you that the dog needs to be listening too on a visit.

9

~6~

Finding Medical Equipment on Your Own

Let's face it, not many people have wheelchairs, crutches, walkers and the like lying around the house so to get started I suggest you check out your medical supply stores and ask if they have some used equipment they will allow you to use. Check also with churches, Salvation Army stores, and yard sales for equipment, you may have to pay a small fee for it but you can later donate it and claim it on your taxes.

One piece of equipment that you cannot buy and no evaluator will have but you may need to practice with is a security detector, especially if one of your interests is to visit a prison system. For this you can go to your local court house or police station and see if they have the metal detection bars that you can walk the dog through. During prison visits, the dog will be wearing a collar and tags and they may set off the alarm. It's best to know how your dog will handle that sudden sound. Of course there are some sounds that you can't reproduce until you are in the situation, but getting the dog used to as many sounds as possible can greatly help.

~7~

Therapy Dog Testing

Therapy dog organizations have different ideas for testing but many have common denominators. The dog needs to be obedience trained and there is usually an age stipulation for the pet and sometimes for the handler as well. You can see via the organization's website what their tests entail and I strongly suggest you look at the organizations sites because rules, tests, and requirements change frequently. The majority of therapy dog websites will list the actual test so you know what areas your dog will need to train for to pass the test. Over training a dog is always better than under training! Take note though, that there are Therapy Dog organizations that will not state your dog is certified, only that you passed their test. There are also establishments that will take only certified Therapy Dogs.

I will list the better known National Therapy Dog organizations and information at the end of the book. Contact the ones you are interested in for literature. Be aware that when a test is given, it is not in the same place where you have trained your dog. The purpose of training is to show the dog can do fine in any environment, testing a dog in the environment it is already used too is too easy!

While there are several national organizations to choose from they have different criteria, fees, and testing. Therapy Dogs International (TDI) is one of the oldest organizations and their testing was based on the Canine Good Citizen (CGC) test that the American Kennel Club gives, with a few extra steps added by TDI. This test has changed for 2013 and although the basics are still there in what a dog needs to know, the set up is different, however the dog will still be tested around medical equipment.

If such equipment is new to your dog, then once you have purchased or borrowed some leave them in a part of the home the dog must pass through each day so he gets used to it, play games around it with your dog and toss favorite treats near the equipment so the dog has to go close to it. Don't try to introduce it too soon or the dog may become frightened of it. Once the dog sees this intrusive addition to the home is not going to hurt them, then you will slowly introduce it by using it yourself.

Some organizations require your dog be tested with children present doing what kids do best running, jumping and screeching! This is to see how your dog will react around children. However the children do not come in direct contact with your dog during the testing period. Training the dog around nearby schools during recess is a good way to prepare for this test.

Tempting food is also introduced to your dog to be sure the dog knows the command leave it. With some organizations the evaluator will use a special dog treat and tell you with your dog in a heel position, to walk past it or over it on the floor, while others may ask that the dog be handed the treat by the evaluator. In some cases real human food is used.

Your dog will likely be tested around other dogs/pets and people which it does not know. They may come in close proximity to your dog, within 2 feet, so keeping your dog well-socialized to the public while training is the best way to get them acclimated to all kinds of people and pets. Even though my concentration here is on dogs I say pets because some therapy groups allow cats, rabbits, and other small animals.

Some tests require loud noises to be made nearby such as the dropping of or clanging of pans. They may also require another person to bump into you from the back, or touch the dog a little roughly as if they have no control over their body as one might do who has a neurological or muscular condition.

Delta Society is another National Therapy Dog organization and their testing is a bit different. Delta society will work with you as far as evaluating whether you and the dog are good candidates for therapy, how to safely guide your dog through a visit, the specific needs of clients, how to interact with clients, the facility health and safety codes, and client confidentiality.

Delta has pet partner training courses for a fee, as well as home study courses, but they state specifically that they do not train your dog in obedience. They test for a team's skill and aptitude. One difference between Delta Society and Therapy Dogs International (TDI) when testing is that at the present time Delta requires all dogs to wear specific equipment such as a Halti collar, martingale collar, or harness during an evaluation, whereas TDI feels your dog should be well enough trained that no special equipment need to be worn during testing or on visits.   TDI wants nothing other than a buckle collar, snap collar, or a standard harnesses to be worn during an evaluation or on actual therapy visits.

   It is my opinion that if you need to use training aides then your dog is probably not trained well enough or the dog does not enjoy what you are asking of it. There are very well behaved dogs out there that are perfectly happy with the life they lead within the family unit only, so be very aware of any changes in personality in your dog as this can be a clue that Fido is not interested. For example, if Fido runs away from you the moment you pick up the leash, that's a sign!

   Physical disabilities of a pet are also taken into consideration. Delta Society will have the pet's veterinarian and the pet's owners partake in the decision if the animal is able to participate without pain. TDI wants a clean bill of health from your vet as well, and until 2013, deaf dogs were not allowed to be therapy dogs but they have since changed that and the testing for deaf dogs. Tests are always changing this is why I suggest you always check an organization's website.

   In general, all animals must have a health screen done before they are allowed to participate in any therapy work, no matter which organization you go with. Most organizations require a yearly health screen, but how they test may vary from group to group as many new regulations can be attributed to an incident with a past member. Most of these groups carry insurance on your dog when they are acting as Therapy Dogs, hence part of your yearly fee, so any incidents reported may make for a rule change, right down to health screening.

   The two agencies listed above are better known, but there are others that are national as well.

When it comes to an evaluation, not all organizations are alike. Love on a Leash Therapy Dog Club requires you to have a professional dog obedience instructor/trainer/behaviorist or vet fill out a form on the basic obedience and temperament your pet displays when the pet is put in certain situations, such as when a stranger approaches. The test makes no mention of testing around medical equipment, but does ask that a team form be filled out by a supervisor who has observed the team together for at least five visits to a total of ten hours of supervised visits.

The person supervising can be another dog team with the group or the activities director of the facility. It also approves other animals for therapy work such as cats and rabbits.

Therapy Dogs, Inc. (not to be confused with Therapy Dogs International) makes observations of the dog/handler team at a minimum of two medical facilities and a maximum of four, as well as general observations on how much control the handler has on the dog and how the dog interacts with other people and dogs. The owner is also observed in the way they present themselves, personality and personal grooming, and how they treat their dog for poor and good behavior.

Therapets require that you and the dog take an outside obedience class of your choice for 6 to 8 week sessions and you are required to pass the American Kennel Club's Canine Good Citizen test. From there you sign up to take the Therapet Skills Class. The skills classes run for seven weeks and there is a cost. This course teaches you and your dog all the skills you will need to begin volunteering. At the end of those seven weeks your instructor will know if you are ready to be tested. This particular organization does not publically post their test as other organizations do so that when they test a dog they know they are getting a first hand reaction, not something the owner has practiced with the dog or trained for. Once you pass the test then you may volunteer at the place of your choice but under supervision and there is a probation period. Therapet also requires a yearly skills 'check off' to be sure the volunteer team (dog/handler) is maintaining their training level. Also, the handler must attend an annul re-orientation which is separate from the annual skills check off. Personally, as a trainer I think this is a great idea.

Bright and Beautiful Therapy Dogs test is very similar to the Therapy Dogs International test, which includes basic obedience and being tested around other dogs and medical equipment. As with Therapy Dogs international, food is introduced to your dog and the dog is required to leave it upon command.

Fees:

Testing fees range in price from year to year and from organization to organization. Some are as little as ten dollars per test whether you pass or fail and others are higher if there is a sponsoring club involved, meaning that that club may charge a fee to use their facility to do the test as well. Do not get the testing fee confused with the yearly team fee to belong to the organization. Fees are charged per team and can run from forty dollars per year to one hundred and ninety dollars a year so you definitely want to check the fees of each club.

If there are two or three people in the family that want to do visits with the dog as well then yearly fees are required for those persons also although it may only be portion of the original team fee. Therapet states it does not charge a yearly fee, although there is some cost in the items needed to buy for your pet to show it is a Therapet.

Speaking from my own experiences as an evaluator and as a dog trainer for many years, in a perfect therapy dog world, I would agree with and combine many of the tests from the various groups in this book, but what I would really want to see for all groups is a retest for each team, if not annually then at the very least every three years. Why? Because people's lives change, they get lax, and the dog is sometimes taken out of regular training and therapy visits. Also dogs tend to go through behavior changes at specific ages, and in some cases those changes are due to health problems that would not be picked up with the ordinary vet checks that are required today. Dog breeds also age differently, so whereas a Newfoundland reaches its senior years at age four, a Cocker Spaniel doesn't see senior years until possibly age ten. There are so many variables and it is impossible to isolate one group of dog that may have more health problems as they age, but a retest could put things in perspective for the safety of the dog and for the owner as well. Sometimes even though our dogs really love doing something, it doesn't mean they should be doing it.

~8 ~

Picking a Therapy Dog Group

There are certainly plenty of local dog therapy groups to join. Local groups are usually affiliated or spin offs of national organizations and require you to pass all the testing standards that the affiliated national group puts forth.

    If you are tested and join a national group only, there is more of a possibility that it will be up to you to find places and make visitation arrangements, but some people prefer to be on their own. National groups list their upcoming testing dates and sites on their webpage or you can call them to find the next testing date and place in your area.

    Local groups adhere to the rules and testing requirements of their affiliate national group and in many cases they have evaluators within their group to give your dog the test needed, or they bring in evaluators for a specific date to test dogs. All dog testing is open to the public but there may be limitations as to how many dogs can be tested on that date, so always call and make an appointment when you are ready to take the test.

    If you go with a local group there are usually benefits that go along with a membership. Local organizations are more likely to have set dates and places for the group as a whole to visit.

This does not mean you have to go on every visit, but the local organizations are more likely to have a variety of places and times they visit to fit your schedule. The head of a local group deals with the third party at a facility to get dates which best serve both the dog group and the facility. Local groups also usually have newsletters, national club updates, fun outings, and fundraisers that are strictly for their group. As well, they may offer a site where you can keep up with the dog's training year round. Local groups may charge a membership fee and this can vary depending on if they need to rent space to do weekly trainings or testing, if they provide literature, purchase equipment, and so on. The benefits you and the dog will get through joining a local group usually outweigh the cost of the membership. Regardless of which you decide, your dog is covered by insurance through the national group, but you will be doing most of the leg work of calling the Activities Director and setting up appointments for visits.

The places you can visit are endless. If you enjoy the antics of children, call your local schools or preschools and see if you can do a Read to Dogs program, or do a program about bite safety. Some libraries have also started story time with a Therapy Dog periodically so be sure to talk to them as well.

Thoughts from an Evaluator's Perspective

Although I have been training dogs for over twenty years and have used many methods old and new to train, as an evaluator I have to step back from a trainer's standpoint and strictly evaluate a team for therapy work. This is sometimes very hard to do, but once the test is done I can then offer advice on other ways to handle a situation that may have been the cause of failure. A good example of this is when I was asked to test a retired search and rescue dog.

Hmm, I thought, *how hard could an already well trained dog be to test?*

Boy was I ever wrong! The dog was well trained in search and rescue so he was used to being on a long lead or off lead totally and away from his handler's side which made it very difficult for the owner to get the dog to heel! The poor dog was confused as to what it was being asked to suddenly do after years of working in the fields off lead. Needless to say I had to fail the dog as it was great at search and rescue but did not handle the commands needed to pass a therapy test.

Throughout the testing the owner kept making mention that the dog was used to being away from her side and that even taking the dog for a leisurely walk down the road was difficult. Once the testing was done, my trainer mode kicked in and thoughts began to churn in my head. I suggested that she use different apparatus than what she used when the dog did search and rescue as opposed to when she expected it to have different manners as a therapy dog. For search and rescue she used a harness, for obedience I suggested she start training with a collar and bandanna so the dog knew which job he was supposed to do for her at that moment.

Dogs are smarter than we give them credit for. Generally it is human error that causes our dogs to not be the best that they can be. The women contacted me several weeks later via email and stated that the dog was doing better with different attire.

I do believe I have failed more teams than I passed over the years, basically because those well behaved and happy dogs at home are just that, happy and well behaved at home not necessarily when brought out into strange and unfamiliar places.

As an evaluator, when I hear the handler make excuses for the dog's behavior during a test, it sends a red flag that maybe this dog has not been in the public among strangers and other animals often enough but is probably a dog that is very polite at home and mostly visits other family members and other family dogs.

I liken this type of person to the old Italian griever. You know, the Italian woman all dressed in black clutching Rosary beads in her hand at the ready to throw herself on top of the coffin as they lower it into the ground? It does not stop until the body is covered, similar to the excuses the owner's give me throughout the test as to why their dog is not doing what is asked of it.

When I come across this type of team, I don't stop the test right away, I usually give the team an extra chance and I do this because I want the owner to realize that even with repeated prompts the dog does not comply. My reason for doing this comes from years of failing owners who just could not quite understand where the problem lay, and in turn would get angry with me for not giving a second, third, fourth and fifth chance! By doing it this way I can point out to the owner when the test is over that I had given the team several tries and because of that they are more likely to be open about the problem. But take note, if and when the dog finally comes around and listens maybe on the fifth try, it does not mean the dog passes that portion of the test!

There are many reasons that a team might fail or be immediately dismissed from taking a test and each organization put their own rules into effect regarding this so I will go over some of the reasons for the group I am affiliated with.

Immediate dismissal
- The dog is not yet one year of age.
- The dog acts aggressive to another animal or person while waiting to take the test or during any part of the test.
- The dog is wearing any type of training apparatus
- The owner is seen giving harsh punishment to a dog.
- Ill health of a dog
- The handler is ill tempered or not of good character
- The team belongs to another therapy dog organization

- The dog is a certified service or assistance dog
- The handler is under the age of 18 with no accompanying adult

Most common reasons for failure during testing:

- The dog shies/pulls away/lunges or barks at the evaluator or at equipment during testing.
- The dog urinates during testing inside a facility.
- The dog struggles to take the food during the Leave it phases.
- The dog needs repeated prompts to obey a command.
- The dog growls /barks at evaluator or other dogs.
- The dog barks/whines/pulls during the supervised separation portion.
- The dog panics/barks/ acts aggressive during reaction to distractions phase.
- The dog shows ill health/pain during any part of the test.
- When walking on a loose lead, the dog is not near the owner's leg.

~10~

Tips from an Evaluator

The tips I would give are these:

1) Be honest with yourself and take your dog to *various* places and see how well the dog listens to your commands. If you need to give 3, 4 or 5 verbal prompts then the dog is not ready for therapy work.

2) RELAX! This is not the Spanish inquisition! You are not going to be banished from the Therapy Dog kingdom! At the very most you may fail a portion of the test and need to retake it at a later date. There is no shame in that, best efforts are better than no efforts! Usually it is the most nervous person who is worried about doing it right that passes the test and all that nervousness was for nothing!

3) Come early for a test, up to half hour early and let the dog get familiar with the atmosphere around it. Let the dog get familiar with the other dogs, people and equipment at the testing site, this helps them get that excitement out of the system so they are free to focus on your commands and not worry what the other dogs are doing. Introduce yourself to those around you as this will help you take the edge off.

4) Once the dog's excitement is out of the way and you are in a calmer state of mind, start working with the dog in a few commands so there is an understanding that this is the time to be listening to your commands.
Don't fret! At first the dog will not listen to you at all or will only listen briefly, when it counts they'll probably do fine.

5) For many, taking the test is a bit nerve wracking only because most don't like to fail. This can turn a normally calm, easily adaptable person straight into a clumsy ox that cannot suddenly walk or hear the instruction the evaluator gives! We understand that, so don't be afraid to ask for something to be repeated, we do not take offense or get upset over this, in fact we actually admire it because it shows that you as the handler want to do it right.

6) Prepare, prepare, prepare! There is nothing more frustrating than an owner who may very well have a perfect therapy dog in the making but they are not prepared for the test, so be sure to read each site's testing requirements and be prepared.

7) Stop making excuses throughout the test as to why you believe the dog may not be listening to you. If the dog is not compliant just ask if you can take the test at a later date so you have time to work on the issues.

8) Never punish your dog for any mistakes as that alone can be a reason for dismissal. Dogs are dogs, they're not perfect, but their hearts are big and punishment from the owner can take that big heart down a size or two. We want the dog to remain that same loveable way that made you think it would make a great therapy dog to begin with!

~11~

Training for Success!

As stated earlier, almost all national Therapy Dog organizations list their tests on their website or have brochures. I strongly suggest that you look over each one and compare the testing as well as other benefits of the club. All organizations require your dog have basic obedience which means upon command the dog should be able to sit, stay, down, come, heel, left turn, right turn, about turn, halt, and leave it.   You can get this training in any basic obedience class however no two trainers are alike in their training methods or ideology. There are trainers who use the older method of the correction of the choke chain or prong collar with or without treats as reward, there are those that use clicker training and there are those that just use their voice and there are some that combine many methods. It is up to you to pick the training method you are comfortable with. Fees for training vary and like everything else it is going to depend on the person you choose and possibly where you live. A trainer in a rural community may not charge as much as a trainer in a City. One who trains a full class together is not going to be more than one that trains you individually.

Of course it is perfectly fine for you to not take any classes and train the dog yourself in your own way. Just decide beforehand what group you are going with so you know what is expected of the dog.

I believe as a trainer that one's dog should be rewarded for its efforts and should want to be with you, if you can keep those two thoughts in your mind your dog should succeed!

~12~

Training the Commands

Using the Clicker Method

Before I get into clicker training, when training at home on your own, all new commands should be taught in a quiet non distracting area. Once the dog has learned the commands you can start to bring the dog to places that have distractions. Always keep a leash attached to your dog when you train outside. Start training commands in the home and then progress to other areas such as a garage or yard; gradually introduce other areas that present more distractions such as the street in front of your home then to the park etc. If at any time your dog ignores commands that have already been learned then you need to return and work the dog longer in the area where it last succeeded.

Here is a list of what you will need to get started.
1. A clicker (sold in the majority of pet stores)
2. A treat bag that hangs on your belt (or a fanny pack)
3. A six foot and 15 to 20 foot leash.
4. Reward. This is up to you as some dogs are not food motivated so then you would use whatever motivates them which can be a favorite toy.

All of my dogs began training as puppies and were very food motivated which made it easy. I always started with slivers of hot dogs, and then during harder tasks such as the recall (come) phrase I upped the ante to chicken slivers. Some people use dog liver treats, cheese chunks, or cheerios. Whatever you pick as the food reward it has to be something small enough and soft enough that the dog can wolf it down without chewing it. Many make the mistake of using hard biscuits. Biscuits have to be chewed and pieces crumble to the floor which takes the dog's attention off of you which is what you don't want.

"How does the dog know that the clicker sound is good and something good follows that?" You ask.

This short training session will teach your dog the sound of the clicker and what happens after the magical sound appears. What's even better is that you are only saying your dog's name to get their attention. There are no frustrating commands to follow in loading the clicker!

With Clicker training, 40% of time is spent with the dog trying to figure out what you want from it and 60% percent is required patience from you waiting for the dog to complete the desired command. The question is do you have patience to wait the dog out? That is where most people give in and try to force a dog into a position which can get you nowhere, so if you find yourself at that point stop training immediately!

I always compare my dog's mind to that of a young child, if what they do does not make you see the humorous side of their developing minds, then maybe dog ownership is not for you! And you may want to think twice before having kids!

A) Loading the clicker:

Call your dog's name and the moment the dog gives you their attention click and treat. Repeat this several times until you no longer have to call the dog and only the clicking gets their attention. Once this step is accomplished your dog is ready to begin other trainings. Should your dog be afraid of the clicker noise, try putting it in your pocket to muffle the sound. There are also different sounding clickers available; some are softer than others so pick up a few with softer sounds as well. If the clicker still presents a problem then use your voice as the marker with one word, "yes."

B) Eye contact:

Making eye contact is important as it indicates your dog is paying attention. You want to make yourself a leader that your dog will enjoy following. Start out by calling the dogs name and the moment the dog looks at your face click and treat. When the dog does this regularly you are ready to move on to the next command.

If your dog has trouble with eye contact and you may find this in some dogs who are shy or frightened , what you want to do is show the dog the treat, call the dogs name and slowly move the treat right up to your eyes, The dog will more than likely follow the treat as that in itself is not a challenging move as is direct eye contact.

Some pups are small so getting eye contact may be easier if you put them on a table and raise them to your height.

C) Sit:

Sit is the easiest command to teach a dog, however you must remember that sit is a stand alone command. Many people mistakenly say "Fido, sit down." The dog looks at you stupidly as if asking the question, *"Do you want a sit or a down?"* Sit and down are two different commands and should be used as such. To begin, you should not say any command to the dog. Hold the treat over your pet's head as your dog looks up at the treat a natural sit position should occur. As soon as your pet's bottom starts to hit the floor click and treat. Once the dog gets the idea of a sit, make sure the next time before you click that his bottom is planted firmly on the floor. Repeat this process adding the dog's name and the command 'sit'. (Example: Fido, Sit.) The hand signal/command for sit is simply raising your hand up from your waist to your chest area, palm facing up. You can incorporate the vocal command and the hand command in conjunction. As it pertains to any command make sure your voice tone is at normal pitch and not a frustrated tone. If your dog has trouble with a sit in an open area, try putting him as close to a wall as possible so the only alterative is to sit. (*Helpful hint: If you have your dog sit before feeding, petting, answering the door, or greeting you at the door, he will be less inclined to jump on people.*)

D) Release:

Whenever you teach a dog a command it is very important to also give a release command. This tells the dog that the command is over. You can use a short phrase such as the dog's name and 'okay' in a semi exited voice. (Example: Fido, okay!) Always remember to release the dog from a command. You will get longer stays if there is a release command.

E) Down:

Putting your dog in the down position may take a little more work. Dogs feel very vulnerable in the down position so it is important to take more time with this command.   While your dog is in the sit position, put the treat to their nose and slowly bring the treat down toward the floor near their front paws. As the dog's nose follows the treat, drag the
treat on the floor toward you and away from the dog. As the dog follows the treat his front legs should start to move down toward the floor, *click and treat*. Repeat this until you can get the dog's whole body down on the floor. Once they have learned to put their whole body on the floor incorporate the command down. (Example: Fido, down). The hand signal/command is done by starting with your right hand, palm down, just under your chest and bringing it down toward the floor ending just below waist level.

F) Heel:

With the dog in a sit at your left side, the leash in your left hand being held about a foot from the dog's collar, hold the treat in your right hand in front of the dog's nose. Hold the treat as close to your left leg as possible, preferably at the knee of your body. Say the dog's name and the command heel. (Example: Fido, Heel) The dog's head should be even with your left leg and should not go ahead of you. If you are a left handed person do the same but on the opposite side. Whether you have the dog heel on your left or right side, always start off walking with the foot on the side you want the dog to heel on. So, if the heel is on the left, start walking with the left foot.   It used to be that all of us dominant right handed people taught their dogs to heel on the owners left side, and for some reasons that still holds true, but for therapy dog work heeling on either side is okay as long as the dog is in a heel and you have control over the dog at all times.

Eventually, as the dog learns what heel means you will hold the leash normally and loosely. When heel is learned correctly there should be a leash loop from the dog's collar to your hand. As an Evaluator if I see you tugging or holding the leash tight with no give or loop on the lead, it tells me a couple of things. A) You are very nervous, B) this is the normal way you walk your dog or C) you don't have control over the dog. So relax and let the leash droop a bit, and since you will be asked at some point in the test to make right turns, left turns, and about turns it is imperative that the dog be in a heel at your side, the dog's head by your knee, the dog should not be too far ahead of you or too far from the side of you.

When you are asked to halt by the Evaluator, the dog should sit at your side in position ready to get up and heel again when prompted. As stated above, heel which is the 'out on a lose lead' portion of a therapy test is where I see much needed improvement with the owner and one of the top reasons for failure by me. You have to think of this loose lead as a possible hazard, if the dog is far from your body the extended leash poses a risk to a resident, so a close heel is imperative.

The hand signal/command for heel is simply stepping off with the foot on the side your dog is heeling with a verbal prompt of the dog's name and heel. That stepping off foot movement will be a visual cue. You can also pat your leg as you step off with the heel foot for an extra visual.

(Helpful hint: If you practice heel in a narrow hallway the dog will have no choice but to stay near you).

G) Sit Stay:

When it comes to the sit-stay or down- stay portion of a therapy dog test, listen carefully as some tests/evaluators require you to call the dog to you when you reach the end of the leash under their instruction, or the evaluator may have you reach the end, wait a minute or two then have you return to the dog. The dog should not break position until you give it a release. Put the dog in a sit command at your side. Holding the leash in your hand, position your other hand/ palm in front of the dog's face, which will be the hand signal and say Fido stay. Step off with the non heel foot and position yourself directly in front of your dog. Remember that if you use your heel foot to step away from the dog, the dog will get the visual cue of heel and may get up, so start with the opposite foot from what the dog's visual cue for heel is. Example, if you heel on the left side you would step away from the dog with your right foot, then turn, step in front of the dog and face the dog. Stand about one foot or less in front of the dog repeating the dog's name and the command stay. Wait only a few seconds at first, if the dog stays, give the release command (Fido okay!) click and treat. Gradually you will increase the distance between you and the dog and the amount of time of the stay. Try to always catch their good behavior in the stay command by clicking and treating before the dog has a chance to get up and break the stay. Always remember to give your pet the Okay release command. This in the long run helps the dog to stay longer. As you start to work on stay commands you want to invest in a 20 foot cotton training lead so you can gradually increase the distance between you and your dog but the dog will still be attached to a lead for safety.

Should the dog break the stay, don't click and treat as it is not the behavior you asked for, just say 'oops' in a non threatening tone, place them back in the initial spot in the sit position and shorten the stay time and build from there

H) Down Stay:

Put the dog in the down position at your side. Put your hand in front of the dog's face and give the stay command. Step off with your opposite heel foot. Again going only about a foot in front of him and repeating the command stay. Remember to click and treat for good behavior. Follow the above steps as you did in sit/stay, gradually increasing the time and distance between you and the dog. The down- stay position is the most difficult for the dog to perform as it feels very vulnerable and open to attack. Should the dog break the down stay, just say "oops" in a non threatening tone and start again at the place where the dog broke the down command. You may also want to step on the leash to prevent the dog from getting up. This will only work if you are close to the dog but it is a start in getting a good stay. Just remember to release, click, and reward.

While all dogs should be taught a good down and sit stay there are groups that omit rescued Greyhounds from performing this so be sure to ask before you test what the organizations rules are regarding Greyhounds.

At present, the Greyhound is not released from this part of the CGC test. Greyhounds can learn the sit and down stay, though it may require a longer training period and lots of patience.

I) Wait:

Sometimes an evaluator may ask you to put your dog in a wait when what he/she really means is to put your dog in a stay. This is usually nothing more than different terminology being used by the evaluator. Please be sure to clarify what the evaluator wants, a stay or a wait.

What is the difference between stay and wait?

The stay command means to the dog to stay where you are until you are released. A wait command may be given if your hands are full of groceries and you are trying to get through the door before your dog pushes past you knocking all of the groceries to the floor! When I teach wait I use the hand sign of human sign language which is to put your right hand to the left shoulder and wiggle the fingers. This action makes the dog look up at your shoulder waiting for the fingers to stop so it keeps the dog's attention. Using this hand sign to teach wait will also help the dog know that the hand you put in front of the its face means stay until I tell you what I want you to do next, where as this simple hand sign at the shoulder is at different height and means something else entirely. Many trainers do the hand in front of the dog's face for stay and wait which can sometimes be confusing to the dog and this is why many dogs break a stay.

Training Wait

To teach wait, bring the dog to a quiet room, have the dog sit, face the dog and say the word wait while giving the human sign gesture simultaneously. Keep the dog there for only a few seconds at first, then drop your hand and turn away from the dog. At this point your dog will wonder what's going on, no click, no treat? Take a step or two away from the dog and call the dog to you. When the dog gets by your side click and treat. By clicking after you've turned around and in movement when then the dog is called to your side, you are rewarding the whole behavior of waiting briefly. Once the wait command is learned by the dog you will not need to give the sign at the shoulder at all times because let's face it, you can't walk through a door with an arm full of groceries and give a hand gesture! This is why I suggest that you continue to move with your back to the dog and then call the dog.

If you have a bubbly dog who just can't wait to get into the house then another way to teach the wait command while going through a door is to have the dog stand at the door as if you are both going to enter, tell the dog to wait, slightly open the door and as the dog starts to bolt through like there are ants in his pants quickly close the door and repeat the wait command.

You must be careful not to open the door too far or close it too fast, you don't want your fingers getting stuck or the dog's nose to get hurt between the door and door jam. You are just getting a point across that when he acts like that, the door closes and no one gets in. The very minute you see improvement on his wait, then repeat the wait until you can open the door all the way and he will not go through. Step through the door, walk a couple of steps then call him to you, click and treat.

J) Leave it!   The leave it command is very high up on the list of reasons for failed dogs on the therapy test. If your dog does not have a good leave it command down they can actually cause harm to themselves. Residents keep food in their room that can be toxic to dogs such as grapes or raisins. In hospitals, snacks are sometimes taken off a food tray for the resident to have later in the day. Medication dropped on the floor is another area of concern, so getting a leave it command in place is essential. This is a command that you want to practice often in any situation you are in, even during play so the dog is continuously brushed up on this command.   To teach the leave it command, take a boring everyday treat such as a biscuit in one hand, show it to the dog and then throw it on the ground about three feet from the dog. In your other hand you will also have a very special treat such as a piece of chicken. You want to make sure this special treat is one he does not normally train with and something very yummy. Have a leash on the dog and give the command of 'Leave It' to your dog as he eyes the biscuit you just threw on the ground. Show and give the dog a whiff of the better treat in your other hand. The minute the dog takes its focus off the biscuit on the floor click and give the delicious treat from your hand. Do this several times until you see the dog is consistent with leaving the treat on the floor. Gradually start walking the dog around the biscuit in about a three foot radius and each time the dog looks at the biscuit you give the command leave it, if the dog looks back at you, click and give them the better treat in your hand. You want to do this each and every time they look away from the treat on the ground and put their attention back on you when that command is given. You can repeat this command often as you walk around the treat because this is a very tempting and hard command for a dog.

Repeat this process until you are able to put the food on the floor say the command only once and the dog will continuously pay attention to you and not the treat you laid on the floor. The treat in your hand always has to be better than the treat on the floor as the concept you want your dog to learn is that when you give the leave it command and they ignore the food on the floor, that a better treat awaits them for their compliance. However at some point treats will be phased out all together and praise will take its place. This way you're not walking around with a pocket full of chicken! Gradually your goal is to give the command and walk closer and closer to the treat on the floor until you can have the dog walk over top of it without going for it. You also want to teach the dog leave it from a person handing them the treat directly as this is part of some therapy dog tests.

If you feel that tossing the treat on the floor to begin with is just too much for your dog to handle this there is another alternative to start with. Take the boring treat and place it in your right or left hand, have the yummy treat in the opposite hand behind your back and show the dog the boring treat. As the dog goes for it close your hand around the treat making it inaccessible to them. After their sniffing, licking, or pawing at the hand has stopped and they look at you as if to say, *Hey, are you going to give me it or not?* Click and reward with the yummy treat in your opposite hand. Eventually you will incorporate the command leave it and from there you can move to the treat on the ground.

K) Right Turn

This is pretty self explanatory! The Evaluator is going to call out these next few commands as you are in movement so be sure to keep your ears open! By doing these commands it shows the evaluator that you have the dog under control and you will see why when you do the turn which is at the same side of where you heel the dog to your body.

With your dog heeling at your side, the evaluator will call out "Right Turn." You will make a right hand turn with your body and continue walking in that direction while giving the command heel. The dog must follow you through the right turn in the heel position. The dog must not go in any other direction than where your body is facing.

If your dog pulls to go in any other direction this will result in failure of the test because it shows that the owner does not have control over the dog. Though it seems fairly easy I have seen dogs pull to the opposite of where the owner is telling it to go. This is especially important if the test is outside and there are small critters running around.

L) Left Turn

Same as a right turn, as you are moving the evaluator will tell you left turn and you and the dog must head in the same direction. So what's so hard about this? Much of the problem lay with the turn that is on the side of the body in which the dog is heeling on. Since the majority heel on the left side I will explain what I am talking about here. Remember how hard I pounded it into your head about the dog's heel being no further than your knee? Here's the reason. The dog is in a heel at your left side, the dog's head/shoulder area is in front of your knee area and the evaluator calls out "Left Turn!" If the dog's body is too far in front of you, you will be tripping over the dog as you make the turn. Clearly not a huge mistake but you may be reminded of that time you walked down the street and seemingly tripped over nothing feeling embarrassed and wondering, *did anyone see that?*

M) About Turn

An about turn is nothing more than turning your dog and yourself completely around with the dog in the heel position. Example: You and the dog are headed east, the evaluator yells out "About Turn," then you and your dog turn and head west until the next direction is given.

N) Stop/Halt:

Throughout the test, the evaluator will say "Halt" or "Stop" while you are heeling your dog. Your dog must sit beside your heel leg facing in the same direction as you until the command "Forward" is given by the evaluator. Depending on the organization testing the dog, when it comes to Greyhounds the evaluator may not ask for a sit when you stop so be sure the two of you are clear on that.

O) Forward:

Forward means to resume walking with your dog in the heel position. Your dog should not break the sit stay, down stay, or stand stay it was in for the Halt (or Stop) command until you move your leg forward and say heel.

P) Come/Recall:

There are a couple of ways an evaluator might ask you to do the come/recall command. Generally the dog is put in a down stay or sit stay and the owner is asked to walk to the end of a 10 to 20 foot lead and then after a brief time the evaluator will ask the owner to call the dog to them. Any word can be used to get your dog to come, some people say 'Fido Come' some people say 'Fido Here', whatever floats the dog's boat and motivates him/her to respond without many prompts is fine. Language is not a standard so you can teach the dog your commands in any language.

   The command come is the most difficult and takes the longest to teach a dog especially if it is taught in the beginning in the wrong way. What do I mean by that? If you are outside and you call the dog saying "Fido Come" and there is a little gray squirrel in the corner of the yard and Fido is not 100% up on his recall what do you think the dog will respond too, your words or the gray squirrel that looks like tons of fun to chase? Yep, they'll go for the squirrel 98% of the time and over a period of time that this continues to happen, eventually your command come will mean nothing to the dog because the dog has learned not to listen to you. Never give the come command until the dog is 100% reliable with it in every area you teach it.

   The come command as with all commands should start off being taught in a quiet non distracting place so that you are the most interesting thing in the world in that space at that time or at least the one with the most interesting treat in your hand! This is a command where you want to start using soft dog treats inside the home, and as you move to more distracting places you up the ante to the hot dog, chicken and liver. Remember to give only small slivers as a reward and to never give the dog these foods in his dish or they will not be seen as a special reward.

Begin by putting Fido in a sit stay on one side of the room, then call the dog to you and when the dog comes, click and treat. Repeat this process until the dog is familiar with the command come inside the home and at the point when they understand the come command you will start to ask them to come to you and ask for an immediate sit in front of you so that you are facing each other. When the dog is sitting in front of you then that is when you will click and treat. This teaches the dog not only to come to you, but the rest of the command which entails the dog to sit in front of you. When Fido is reliable in every room of the house then you want to move that training to the yard and always on leash. There are lots of distractions in a yard that will take a dog's attention off of you, if the dog becomes distracted when you give the come command, take the leash and start reeling the dog in toward you and at the same time start walking/jogging backward making it a game so the dog stays interested. As the dog nears you, stop, put the dog in a sit then click and treat. You goal is to work up to more and more distracting places, so once taught and understood in the yard, you would move to the driveway and then to the street in front of the home, and then to a park, etc. Always have a reward that would be more enticing than what the dog might desire to go after in more distracting places.

Having several family members in the home to help you make a game out of the command come while inside the home is also a good idea. Each will hold treats and a clicker. Each will call the dog to them. If the dog goes to the person who called it, then the dog gets a click and a treat! If the dog goes to the wrong person that person ignores the dog for a few seconds, at which point the person who originally called the dog calls the dog again. When the dog goes to the right person that person clicks and treats.

When it comes to training, you always want the dog to succeed so it is worth it to the dog to do it repeatedly. If you let the dog fail too many times the dog will become disinterested in the whole ordeal. As well if a training session goes on too long the dog will become disinterested and at times will begin acting out. Always know when to stop a training session and always end it on a good note where the dog succeeds.

If for some reason you have taught the come command previous to reading this book, and the dog is not listening to that command, then you want to start again as described above but change the wording from Fido Come to 'Fido Here!' New beginnings as they say!

A big mistake many owners make with the come command is that on the occasion when the dog does escape and the owner finally catches the dog, the owner scolds it. This is a big no, no! You are teaching your dog that if it comes to you bad things happen. So if your dog happens to get away from you while teaching the come command, never use the command to try and get the dog back as he clearly does not know it well enough, and if by chance you are lucky enough to get the dog back safely to you, give him all the praise in the world and the mother load of treats in your pocket. You never want to make the dog afraid to come to you.

When you have trained outside on a normal leash, then you train again in the same manner with a twenty foot cotton training lead. The cotton lead is used because of its light weight. The light weight makes the dog forget it has anything attached to it and may tend to wander off. When that happens then you call the dog to you but if the dog does not return you can reel the dog in via the lead. This tells the dog that even though it is far from you, you still have control.

Q) Supervised Separation

Part of being a therapy dog is being able to behave when the owner may have to leave a room for a few minutes and the dog has to be left with a friendly stranger. If your dog pulls, whines, or barks so that the stranger cannot calm the dog then the dog will fail the test. There are some dogs that are what we call Velcro dogs and they have a very hard time letting their owner out of site. To train for supervised separation you want to start with a person the dog knows very well and leave the dog with them while you go out of the dog's sight. Start off with only seconds passing before you return and never return when the dog is acting out or the dog will believe that all it need do is act out and you will return to it.

If it happens that the dog is out of control as soon as you leave you are going to have to wait until there is even the slightest calm / quiet before entering the room and returning to the dog. This may take several tries and the wait can be long before some dogs settle down so be sure to get a helper that is fine with a long wait! Gradually you will leave the dog with different people to get the dog used to being without you.

My dog Chance always looked for me when we were out in a crowd so to get him used to being in public without me in his view, my husband and I would take daily walks through town and while my husband held the leash I went ahead and ducked into a storefront. This enabled me to peek through the window and see when Chance was acting less anxious so I could return and reward him. Gradually I increased the time that I was out of sight. When I returned, I brought with me a scrumptious treat, this allowed Chance to associate my being gone with something really good coming his way when I returned. And of course my husband also rewarded good behavior.

~13~

Training Touch for Medical Equipment

I went over a few ways to introduce the medical equipment in the beginning of the book but I would also like to tell you how to use the clicker to get your dog to touch the equipment on command. When your dog does something on command it may be less alienating or frightening to it. Training a dog to target an item can be very helpful to bring a dog closer to a resident who may be in a wheelchair or a bed. What you want to do is start out with a treat in the fist of one hand, the clicker in the other, put the hand with the treat in it out for the dog to smell, as the dog is sniffing your hand click and give the treat. Once the dog gets used to doing that, put the command 'touch' to the hand with the treat in it. You are now training the dog to touch your hand. As the dog becomes reliable with touching your hand start to pick up objects in that hand and ask the dog to touch them, click and treat every time the dog touches an item.

Eventually the dog may get wise to the hand that is holding the treat as just the treat hand so you'll want to switch them up or keep the treats on a counter.

Gradually you will increase the time that the dog is touching an item by adding the command hold. To do this place and even more delectable treat in your hand, if you can stand to, put some peanut butter or cream cheese on the treat, lay your hand on the arm of the couch, closed fist around the treat, ask the dog to touch your hand and the dog will go for the delightful smell of this treat, open your fist just a little so the dog can get its tongue in to taste the covering of cream cheese you applied to it at the same time give the command hold so he learns to hold that position.

Count to five after telling the dog to hold, then click and open your fist for the reward. Gradually you will increase this hold time by counting longer. If by chance you own an active hunting retriever then hold is going to mean something else entirely so then you may want to say touch and wait.

~14~

Phasing Out The Treats:

As your dog learns the commands you will begin replacing treats with praise, however you can continue to use the clicker as a marker that the dog is doing everything right. This marker can be a great help when you begin therapy visits in new places. To phase out treats you will ask your dog to perform a command, click and treat, ask for another command, click and praise, continue this back and forth treat / praise until the dog performs each command even though there is no certainty that a treat is forthcoming. That's it!

~15~

Knowing When to Stop

Just as it is important to know when to end a training session at a time when the dog is succeeding, it is equally important to know when to stop therapy dog visits during the dog's career. I can guarantee you that once your dog starts going on continuous visits it is something that the dog will look forward to each time you attach that bandanna or therapy jacket. Dogs very quickly learn the routine you put them through before going on a visit and they come to love it. However just because the dog loves it, it does not mean it is okay to continue if you see that your dog's health is starting to fail at home. Many dogs are stoic when it comes to pain and they will put that pain aside when they are going to do something that they love. This is where it is up to you to make that decision for your dog and retire the dog at the appropriate time.

~16 ~

The Final Act

"Hello?" Jodi said as she answered the phone.

"Jodi?" I asked. "Can you and Dan come over and help me?"

Jodi could tell by my voice something was not right. "What's the matter?" She asked.

"It's Chance, I said, I need to get him to the vet and I can't move him alone, I think there's something wrong with his back." My tears streamed down my face as I tried to choke back the emotion in my voice.

"We'll be right over." Jodi replied.

As they came through the door it was clear that just picking up this 175 lb dog was not going to happen.

"Do you have an old blanket?" Jodi asked.

My eyes scoured the bedroom and I ripped the bedspread off the bed and laid it on the floor near Chance.

"Come on Chance." Jodi called as she patted the bedspread while Dan lifted Chance's hind end onto the blanket.

Chance struggled to comply and finally we were able to get him onto the bedspread. I could see the frightened look in his face, the confusion as to what was going on, he was used to being the strong one, he was used to being the protector, not the protected.

We hoisted him via the blanket into the back of the van and I thanked my good neighbors for their help and then I quickly set out to the Vet's office. I had believed that Chance may have had a pinched nerve along the spine which is why he could not get up.

Having called ahead, my vet was expecting me and as I pulled into the lot and the Vet Techs brought a stretcher out to the car. Carefully they laid Chance upon it and put straps around his body to secure him and again I could see the fright and confusion in his face.

"It's okay Chance, I said, we're going to get you fixed."

Once we were in the exam room the Vet was able to get Chance to stand and I was thrilled to see this thinking the disc was not ruptured! The Dr. gave him a thorough exam and Chance allowed him to poke and prod.

"I don't think there is a disc problem." The vet said as he examined him further.

He placed his stethoscope on Chance's chest and listened intently. Chance stood there panting which was normal for him at the Vet's office, a place he did not like to be.

"Let me get a sonogram." The Dr. suggested. "I'll be right back."

"It's okay Chance." I said as I sat by his side trying to calm him and keep the panting down to a minimum. "You're gonna' be fine, just relax."

The door opened and in came the vet with the sonogram machine.

He tried to get a picture of Chance's chest but the big lug just had too much hair so that the machine could not get a clear picture.

"You can shave the area down." I said. "He won't be going on any therapy visits for a while."

"No that's okay, the Dr. replied, let me try the EKG."

The doctor hooked Chance up to the EKG and Chance's heart beat was jumping all over the place.

Silly nerves! I thought. *He always gets worked up here.*

"Do you see how his heart rate is jumping up and down like this? The doctor asked. How it goes from one extreme to the other."

"Yes." I said, again thinking it was his nerves.

"It's what is called Atrial Fibrillation, the Dr. said, the heartbeat is not normal.

I knew all to well what that meant as my husband had been through such a problem that year and thankfully medication was able to bring the heart back into rhythm.

"With dogs, the Vet said, even if we give medication they may only live another week. In many cases, A fib leads to heart failure."

My mind could not comprehend what he was trying to tell me, partly because it meant I needed to make a decision, a decision I never wanted to make until Chance was much, much older. He had just celebrated his eighth birthday complete with birthday cake and hats just a few short months ago.

This can't be happening! My mind screamed. *Oh my God, this can't happen, not now!*

I continued to stroke Chance as he lay there with the EKG hooked up to him having a conversation about his life or death, it felt wrong and it hurt me deeply.

"I'm all by myself." I whispered through my tears. "I'm all by myself and I could not get him back here on my own if I needed to."

I could see the sorrow in the Vet's eyes as I made my decision to put Chance down.

"I'm so sorry; the Vet said, there's not much that we can do for them when it concerns the heart like this."

I just nodded my head as there were no words that could make this go away there was only a deep stabbing pain in my own heart and an open hole going through my body like I had been shot at point blank range. As the vet leaned over Chance's big head to unplug the EKG machine Chance outstretched his tongue one last time as the Therapy Dog that he was and brushed the Doctor's cheek.

"Aw, thanks buddy, the Vet said, you're such a good guy."

Chance died October 11, 2011, he left this world having cheated death once when he was born but sadly not to be repeated a second time. He is missed by the many that knew him and because he was the mascot for two counties of the Pennsylvania State Animal Response Team the local paper was nice enough to run his eulogy.

For me, life goes on but the pain sometimes seems unbearable, hopefully with time the better memories will erase that awful pain. I don't know if I will ever get to own another dog like Chance given the strong and overwhelming bond we had, but I do know that I was lucky to have shared my life with him.

Chance's Eulogy in the Danville, PA News:

Bloomsburg Fair Favorite Dies

"Are the big black dogs here?" These are the words that would echo through the ears of the Columbia /Montour State Animal Response Team (SART) as they took their usual spot in front of the horse barn at the Bloomsburg Fair for the previous five years.   The big black dogs they referred to were not confined to a cage in the dog show building, or part of the dock dogs, but they are the Newfoundland's known as Chance & Steeler, who positioned themselves in front of the SART trailer waiting anxiously to greet new and old patrons alike to take a picture, grab a pat, or give a kiss, but more importantly to help spread the word of what the Pennsylvania SART organization did. The fairground guards who were stationed at the entrance gate of which Chance & Steeler passed through daily, fondly called these dogs, "The Bears."
It is with a heavy heart that we make the announcement to our patrons that one of our 'bears' has recently passed away. "2nd Chance at Life" who cheated death as a puppy had given his final call on October 11, 2011 when his heart gave out on him.

Chance started his therapy dog career at the age of one doing therapy work with the Susquehanna Trail Dog Training Club through the guidance of the late Dixon Cuff. As time went on Chance was involved in visits to hospitals, special needs children events, early education centers, children's fairs, colleges, nursing homes, the Choir from Uganda, Allenwood Federal Prison visits, and as well he started a Read to Dogs program at the Danville Elementary School. Chance also took part in the making of a cookbook with the proceeds going to aid Newfoundland dogs around the USA.

At the age of two when Chance became the mascot for the Columbia/Montour County Animal Response Team, he attended different events to bring public awareness about the important role the SART organization played for our family pets. Soon he and the words Columbia/Montour SART became synonymous. During his years as the SART mascot, a children's coloring/story book was produced about him. The story teaches young children how to put a pet safety suitcase together for their own pets in case of a disaster. This book is still given out free to children at SART events.

As Chance's owner, I will never forget all the people and places that benefitted from one of his visits, nor will I forget the people we met along the way who spoke so fondly of him. He will be greatly missed.

~17~

Resources

Therapy Dog Listings

Below are the names of the groups I have mentioned with address, phone number and websites. If you have access to a computer you can find many more listings inside and outside the United States. Refer to the link below.
Therapy Dog Organizations.
Net **http://www.therapydogorganizations.net/**

Therapy Dogs International
88 Bartley Rd
Flanders NJ 07836
Phone 973 252 9800
Email **tdi@gti.net**
Link: **http://www.tdi-dog.org/**

Delta Society
875 124th Ave NE #101
Bellevue WA 98005
Phone 425-679 -5500
Link http://www.deltasociety.org/

Therapy Dogs Inc.
P O Box 20227
Cheyenne WY 82003
Phone 877- 843-7364

49

Email therapydogsinc@questoffice.net
Link http://www.therapydogs.com/

Therapets
PO Box 130118
Tyler Texas 75713
Phone: 903 535 2125
Link http://www.therapet.com/ There is a form on the page to send an email
directly

Bright & Beautiful Therapy Dogs
80 Powder Mill Road
Morris Plains, NJ 07950

Phone 973-292 3316
Toll free 888 PET-5770
Email Info@Golden_Dogs.org
Link http://www.golden-dogs.org/

Love on a Leash
PO Box 4115
Oceanside CA 92052-4115
760- 740- 2326
Email info@loveonaleash.org
Site http://www.loveonaleash.org/

In Memory of Chance

A touch

A touch generates a smile
A touch inspires laughter
A touch softens a heart
A touch eases the pain
A touch elicits a listening ear
A touch strengthens a mind
A touch awakens the spirit
A touch is sometimes hard to find.
To be touched lies within the soul
Of every Therapy Dog

By Sally Grottini

Steeler and Chance under their billboard

Steeler & Chance~ County Animal Response Team
Teams which aide animals during a disaster.

College Visit
Therapy Dogs are used in colleges to relieve
stress during exam time or to comfort
students away from home for the first time.

Preschool visits can aide special needs children or
Teach kids about bite prevention

The Susquehanna Trail Dog Training Club trains year round in obedience. Continued training in a group setting keeps dogs socialized with people and other dogs which is very important for Therapy Dog work.

Made in the USA
San Bernardino, CA
09 May 2015